BRAVE ENOUGH
TO BE AFRAID

Best Wishes,

BRAVE ENOUGH TO BE AFRAID

D. Martyn Heath

APEX PUBLISHING LTD

First published in 2004 by
Apex Publishing Ltd
PO Box 7086, Clacton on Sea, Essex, CO15 5WN, England

www.apexpublishing.co.uk

British Library Cataloguing-in-Publication Data
A catalogue record for this book
is available from the British Library

ISBN 1-904444-20-2

Typeset in 16pt Baskerville

Cover Design Jenny Parrett

Printed and bound in Great Britain

To my superior equal

This book is meant to be a book of guidance,
a friend even.
Something we turn to in times
of need and problems.
It is meant to be a starting point, a first
step forward, a gentle push of motivation that we all
need sometimes,
to get our life rolling again.
I hope the bridge of friendship founded in this book
never cracks.
- D. Martyn

I know of no man's disability,
any greater or lesser than mine,
which hasn't taught him some higher
understanding of himself.

Enjoying the company of others starts
with being comfortable with yourself.

He who ventures out, travel far.
Yet those who venture within,
travel further.

If tomorrow wasn't a certainty...
What would you have to do today?

The wounds that don't mark
always scar the deepest.

Sometimes a step backward
is a look forwards.

Let those around you
serve for illustration through-out life.

Your destiny is not pre-determined,
it is self-chosen.

Why should we only appreciate
what we've lived through?

Most of us will wear many faces
before we choose our own.

Sometimes you have to leave your home,
in order to go and find it.

Existence is a chain of habits.
Be different... Live.

Those that push away
yearn closeness the most.

It's the working towards your dream
which is the achievement...
not the completion of it.

Rejection is better than
acceptance on the wrong terms.

The only real threat we are to ourselves is:
Our ability to doubt our ability.

Problems are only trivial
when they're not your own.

If someone could give you everything...
Would you really take it?

We all want honesty,
but never the truth.

The strength of any man
is not in how much he can lift,
but in how much he can carry.

He who finds a balance between living
and having dreams...
often achieves both.

The fear you've never voiced,
speaks volumes about your silence.

Regret is often born
where the dream arrests.

The inferior aim to be equal.
The superior... never to be.

We all have a place on earth,
yet some of us are more particular
in our seat.

Caution can keep a world away.

Travel your journey with persistence,
not speed.

Prudence never travels with speed.

There is wisdom in innocence
age cannot see.

Inspiration without ambition...
is much like holding up a candle
without a flame.

Nothing is ever permanent...
even the winds direct.

Life goals are all about measurements...
Probable estimates fall short.

The past has brought you up to now...
what will you do
from now on?

Confidence:
Instant high heels.

Life's a lesson.
The difficulty is it's self taught.

In life
we have two simple choices...
Starve yourself of it
or nourish it.

Sadness brings the truth out of friends.

Instinct serves better judgement
than recommendation.

Depending on how you see time...
you either wake with a future
or
have a past.

The best form of communication
is to listen.

Those that set themselves deadlines
will always be conscious of the clock.

Life is about risks.
The one's we take
and the one's we don't.

Fate just may be the smile
you took the time to see.

The world is
never in a rush when you are.

Many humans exceed their limitations
much before their expectations.

There's more to each of us...
than our mere bodies suggest.

Imagination is fundamental to dreams...
no matter what the age!

Patience needs never to be waited
in stillness.

We would observe more
by missing a little television.

Accept yourself.
You are the breed of life.
Part of the greatest phenomenon.

Don't sleep your whole life away
on your feet.

Laughter is not the only form
of happiness.

The mirror reflects
only what the mind
wants to see.

Never let hope
over-compensate creativity.

The true patriotism of self
is inner peace.

Mimic none.
What is life
without your creation?

Better the dreams that grace the grounds
than those that flirt with the stars.

If all days are numbered...
Why don't we make them all count?

There is nothing more uglier
than the look of someone's judgement.

Not all feet
suit every road.

No leap was taken without a fall.

A strong opinion will always be heard
further in distance
than a raised one.

It's easier to commit to an excuse,
than a commitment alone.

Much is learnt from the silence of others.

React to someone's doubt
with a smile of certitude.

Ambidextrous:
The ability to grasp life with both hands.

Today the child learns...
What tomorrow he can teach.

When success, however trivial,
becomes your only priority...
it instantly becomes a failure.

You are the opinion of yourself.
The beginning and the end.

The shadow of any problem is always
bigger than the problem itself.

Those who build walls
never build bridges.

It's not the time that's the quality -
But the person you spend it with.

Much strength is found within
a single weakness.

Compassionate acts
echo through all good men.

Unlike any other wheel,
the wheel of progress is easier
to stop than start.

Even a sleeping conscience
awakes screaming.

The child taught on rules will confine.
The child taught on examples
will magnify.

Righteousness takes a lifetime…
Wickedness - a single act.

Love will not be what you perceive it to be
without first…
nurturing it into being.

You are not special…
Problems lie even at your
neighbour's door.

Wealth isn't in currencies
but in values.

No great leap was taken
without many a step.

The true growth of success
is not measured by how much we have
earned, but in how much we have learnt.

Even darkness comes in many colours.

Love is best served on a compliment.

Failure cannot tolerate persistence.

No one stands to admire the flower,
however delicate she is,
while she's still in bud.
- Open up.

True blindness is the man who can see,
but never notices.

Guidance is the hand that never steers.

You are the judge and jury
to every decision you make or decide.

The man that always talks and never
listens, understands nothing more
than the little he knows about himself.

It is often in solitude,
we find ourselves listening the most.

Life is much like a piece of paper...
we can draw from it
what we like.

Failure will greet every human
on their route to success.

Don't let your last sunset...
be your first.

Things that are taken for granted
are greatly missed.

To drop one's guard
is to lift one's mask also.

It's the freedom you give others to leave,
that makes them want to return.

Your potential is much like a never ending
piece of elastic…
it will expand as far as you are
willing to pull.

A good deed
should never be given on reason.

With every corner
a new direction awaits.

We are all blessed with riches
wealth cannot afford.

It takes everybody's ability
to fully appreciate what is best yours.

Without actions...words speak brief.
Without words...
some actions are never heard.

If you need a reason to get up
in the morning,
have this as your reason...
The world without you, is a world
that will always be wanting.

Opportunities seldom occur
whilst awaiting the knock.

Counselled problems are
cancelled problems.

No one can live your life better.

No man can see the world
from the sight of his doorstep.

It may take many chips
and many progressions to sculpt
the real you.

If years be chapters and life be the story…
Then dearest author…
write yourself well.

It's not the field we are forced to grow in
which attracts people to us,
but the person we ourselves flourish into.

Life is much like a game of chess,
to master at it,
it needs to be played over time.

Life is a calm river…
without a purpose,
you'll just swim aimlessly
to your death.

Some grasp and snatch within their reach.
Others stretch for more.

A great influence never sleeps.

The beauty of leaves is...
they can be turned over
again and again.

Stubbornness never gives you
much room to move.

Those that come across over powering
never weigh much in strength.

Insecurity retains endless aptitudes.

To suffer life takes far greater courage
than to live life.
- So why punish yourself?

You can pace your room
or run the world entirely,
but you still won't clear yourself
of your place at mind..
without facing it.

If any callous person wishes
to compensate himself of his troubles...
He'll need look no further than towards
the hardship of others.

Hope above all, is a precarious custom:
It gives the impression we hold
onto something what we
haven't even grasped.

Any form of humanity,
however short or attentive,
should only part with our
hearts entwined.

Rarely does any argument cease
without kicking up a little dust.

All knowledge must be spent...
No man is his wisdom alone.

Knowledge will give you
your first foot hold only.
Ambition: the ladder.

Ill-fate will burden itself at the bottom
of every door...
no matter if varnished with
wood or gold.

What time is to healing...
Listening is to education.

Gratitude is never taught alone.

Health is a privilege
we sadly only appreciate in sickness.

Love is a virtue
that rewards honesty.

We are far more fortunate
than we know.

The finest of teacher's
is always a student in his own class.

Don't walk round
what you can step over.

Have you ever wondered
where you're running to?

It's easier to accept your disabilities
than it is to endure them.

Pursue your life.
Proclaim your stars
at your own will.

The tragedy of any illness is…
it doesn't just affect the body it violates.

Much independence
depends on
the independence of others.

Never carry the company
of an insult.

Mental shackles
tire minds.

Life is a love worthwhile.

Ghosts never retire
without being put to rest.

Rather the sticks that sting...
than the names that engrave.

A youth of any worth
should exercise outside its boundaries.

The sun always rises.

This book should close
on a new dawn.

With thanks to:
my twin... *Jason*
my mother... *Sharon*
my grandparents... *Ivy & Stanley*
& of course, my love... *Lisa*